curious?about

CODING WITH LEGO

BY JILL SHERMAN

AMICUS LEARNING

What are you

curious about?

Curious About is published by
Amicus Learning, an imprint of Amicus
P.O. Box 227, Mankato, MN 56002
www.amicuspublishing.us

Editor: Ana Brauer
Series Designer: Kathleen Petelinsek
Book Designer and Photo Researcher: Emily Dietz

Library of Congress Cataloging-in-Publication Data
Names: Sherman, Jill, author.
Title: Curious about coding with LEGO / by Jill Sherman.
Description: Mankato, MN : Amicus Learning, [2026] | Series: Curious about coding | Includes bibliographical references and index. | Audience term: Children | Audience: Ages 6–9 | Audience: Grades 2–3 | Summary: "What is Lego Spike? Learn about coding and programming with LEGO Education in this question-and-answer book for elementary readers. Includes table of contents, glossary, books and websites for further research, and index"— Provided by publisher.
Identifiers: LCCN 2024048332 (print) | LCCN 2024048333 (ebook) | ISBN 9798892004978 (library binding) | ISBN 9798892005517 (paperback) | ISBN 9798892006057 (ebook)
Subjects: LCSH: Computer programming—Juvenile literature. | LEGO toys—Juvenile literature. | LEGO Education (Firm)—Juvenile literature.
Classification: LCC QA76.6115 .S5285 2026 (print) | LCC QA76.6115 (ebook) | DDC 005.13—dc23/eng/20250122
LC record available at https://lccn.loc.gov/2024048332
LC ebook record available at https://lccn.loc.gov/2024048333
Photo Credits: Alamy Stock Photo/Niels Quist, 4; Shutterstock/AlesiaKan, cover, 1, 2, 3, 5, 6–7, 11, 12–13, 14, 15, 18, 21, Inside Creative House, 20, LightField Studios, 2, 8–9, Nestor Rizhniak, 16–17, Tsuguliev, 19; The Noun Project/Lewis K-T, 22, 23

Photo Credits: Alamy Stock Photo/Niels Quist, 4; Shutterstock/AlesiaKan, cover, 1, 2, 3, 5, 6–7, 11, 12–13, 14, 15, 18, 21, Inside Creative House, 20, LightField Studios, 2, 8–9, Nestor Rizhniak, 16–17, Tsuguliev, 19; The Noun Project/Lewis K-T, 22, 23

CHAPTER ONE

What is LEGO Education?

LEGO Education makes learning to **code** fun. It teaches kids to build and **program** robots using LEGOs. Kits like SPIKE Essential come with fun electronic parts. There's also a special block called a **hub**. You program the hub, and it tells the other parts what to do.

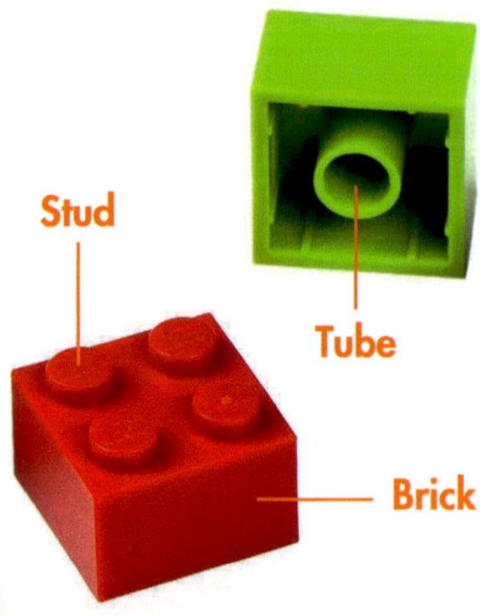

DID YOU KNOW?

LEGO bricks haven't changed much over the years. A LEGO brick from 1958 would still lock with a brick from today!

LEGO's hub lets you turn the robot on and off.

Am I old enough to build a LEGO robot kit?

DID YOU KNOW?

LEGO robotics kits have hundreds of pieces. You'll get motors, sensors, and lights, plus lots of bricks and four minifigures!

Yes! LEGO makes fun robotics kits for all ages. SPIKE Essential is for kids ages six and up. It has all you need to get started building. Want more? SPIKE Prime is for kids 10 and up. It has harder builds. Both kits let you make cool robots!

The kits come with everything you'll need to start building and coding.

You can join an after-school club to learn how to build LEGO robots.

Where can I build LEGO robots?

You can use LEGO kits anywhere. But many teachers love to use the robotics kits in school. They teach a lesson and give instructions. Then students work in groups. They build the robots with LEGO bricks. The last step is to code the robot.

CHAPTER TWO

How does SPIKE work?

SPIKE shows you how to build fun robots. Use bricks to make the robot's body. Add a sensor or motor that lets the robot do cool things. Then, use a computer or tablet to code the instructions. When should the robot move and how? Your code tells the robot what to do.

Building a robot is the first step of coding with LEGO.

Robots cannot move or work without being coded.

Is it hard to code the robots?

Block coding is an easy way to learn to code a robot.

No! LEGO makes coding fun and easy. It uses block coding. You do not need to write hard code. Instead, you can pick colorful blocks. Each block is a bit of code. Stack the code blocks like a puzzle. The robot will follow your instructions!

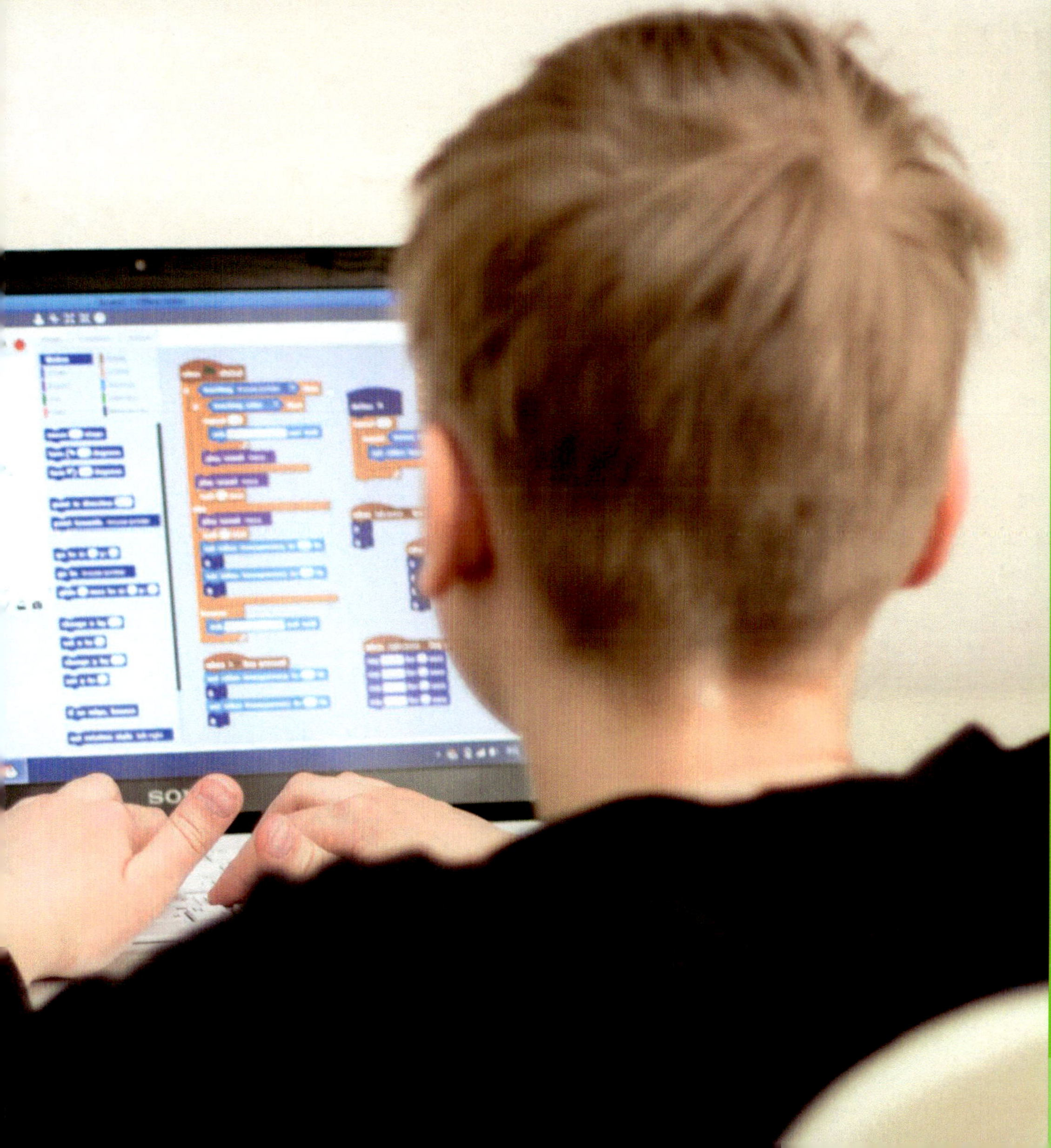

What can LEGO robots do?

So much! It all depends on how you use the parts. Motors and gears let the robots move. With wheels, they can drive. With grippers, they can pick up items. With a color sensor, they can sort your LEGO bricks for you!

UNIQUE BRICKS IN LEGO SPIKE

Gear

Wheel

Ball and Castor

You can make your robot dance by attaching a motor and gears.

Mistakes are a part of the process. Run tests until you can fix it.

What do I do if my robot doesn't work?

Try again! It's okay if your robot doesn't work at first. Testing is a big part of building robots. First, check if the hub is connected. Then, see if the wires are in the right spots. Look at your code and fix any mistakes. Don't give up! You can fix it!

CHAPTER THREE

Do I have to follow the instructions?

You can build anything you can think of.

No! LEGO is all about using your imagination. Once you understand how it works, you can make your own robots. You can mix and match pieces in new ways. Let your creativity fly!

As you get better at building, you can code more advanced robots.

It's easy to share your projects with your family or friends!

How can I share my builds?

LEGO fans are all over the world! There is a great community of builders. Share your creation on a LEGO fan site. You can see what others have made. Maybe you'll find a great idea for your next build!

You can use a tablet or phone camera to take pictures of your builds.

STAY CURIOUS!

ASK MORE QUESTIONS

Can I use LEGO to play games?

How long does it take to build something with LEGO?

Try a BIG QUESTION: What would happen if you used bricks that were not made by LEGO?

SEARCH FOR ANSWERS

Search the library catalog or the Internet.
A librarian, teacher, or parent can help you.

Using Keywords
Find the looking glass.

Keywords are the most important words in your question.

If you want to know about:

- games played with LEGO, type: LEGO GAMES
- how long a kit takes to complete, type: LEGO BUILD TIMES

LEARN MORE

FIND GOOD SOURCES

Here are some good, safe sources you can use in your research.
Your librarian can help you find more.

Books

Block Coding
by Jill Sherman, 2026.

How to Build Lego Robots
by Jessica Farrell, 2024.

Internet Sites

Kiddle: LEGO Mindstorms Facts for Kids
https://kids.kiddle.co/Lego_Mindstorms
Kiddle is an encyclopedia for kids with facts on many topics.

LEGO.com for Kids
https://kids.lego.com/en-us/play
Play games and watch videos about LEGO.

Every effort has been made to ensure that these websites are appropriate for children. However, because of the nature of the Internet, it is impossible to guarantee that these sites will remain active indefinitely or that their contents will not be altered.

SHARE AND TAKE ACTION

Explore other cool LEGO robotics projects.
SPIKE offers dozens of LEGO projects. You can also find more in books or online.

Take your skills to the next level.
Use what you've learned to design your own LEGO robot.

Building your LEGO robotics creations at home?
Bring a completed project to school to show your friends.

GLOSSARY

block code A coding language that uses drag-and-drop blocks to build a program.

code The instructions for a computer program.

hub A central device that joins other devices.

program A set of instructions for a computer to run.

sensor Something that detects heat, light, sound, pressure, motion, or other things.

INDEX

About the Author

Jill Sherman writes books about pop stars, baby animals, and robots. She loves that writing allows her to research and learn about new topics. In addition to writing books, Jill sews her own clothes, creates crossword puzzles, and codes in JavaScript.